Contents

Welcome to Australia!

Hello! My name's Benjamin Blog and this is Barko Polo, my **inquisitive** dog. (He's named after ancient ace explorer, **Marco Polo**.) We have just got back from our latest adventure – exploring Australia. We put this book together from some of the blog posts we wrote on the way.

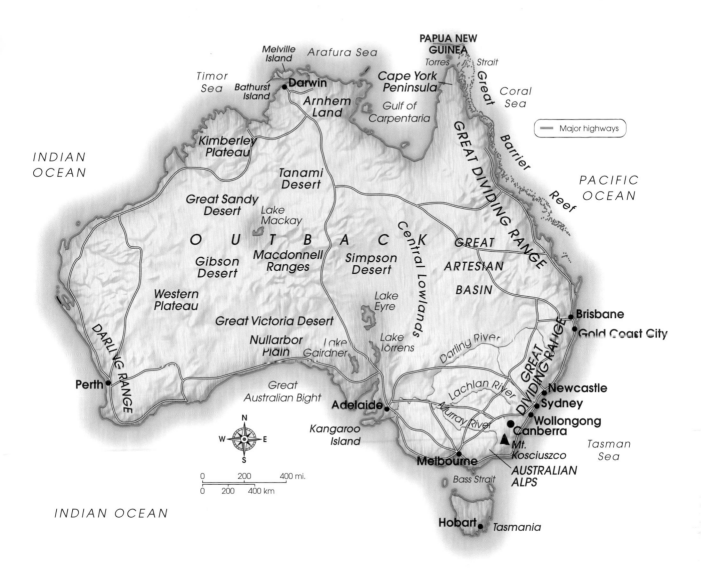

Map labels:

PAPUA NEW GUINEA

Melville Island
Arafura Sea
Timor Sea
Bathurst Island
Darwin
Torres Strait
Cape York Peninsula
Coral Sea
Arnhem Land
Gulf of Carpentaria
Great Barrier Reef

INDIAN OCEAN

Kimberley Plateau
Tanami Desert
GREAT DIVIDING RANGE
PACIFIC OCEAN

Major highways

Great Sandy Desert
Lake Mackay
O U T B A C K
GREAT
Gibson Desert
Macdonnell Ranges
Simpson Desert
Central Lowlands
ARTESIAN
Western Plateau
Lake Eyre
BASIN
Great Victoria Desert
Nullarbor Plain
Lake Gairdner
Lake Torrens
Darling River
Brisbane
Gold Coast City

DARLING RANGE
Perth
Great Australian Bight
Lachlan River
GREAT DIVIDING RANGE
Newcastle
Sydney
Adelaide
Murray River
Wollongong
Canberra
Kangaroo Island
Mt. Kosciuszco
Tasman Sea
N W E S
AUSTRALIAN ALPS
Melbourne
Bass Strait

0   200   400 mi.
0   200   400 km

INDIAN OCEAN

Hobart
Tasmania

BARKO'S BLOG-TASTIC AUSTRALIA FACTS

Australia is a huge island that is also a country. It's surrounded by the Indian and Pacific Oceans. It makes up most of the **continent** of Australia, which is the smallest continent in the world.

The story of Australia

Posted by: Ben Blog | 5 September at 9.43 a.m.

We arrived in Australia and headed straight to Tasmania, an island off the south-east coast. We're visiting the old prison at Port Arthur. This is where criminals were sent from Britain in the 1800s. It's surrounded by shark-infested waters, so the prisoners had no chance of escape.

BARKO'S BLOG-TASTIC AUSTRALIA FACTS

In 1860, Robert Burke and William Wills led the first expedition across Australia. They died on the way back, here at Cooper Creek, from **starvation** and disease.

Rocks and reefs

Posted by: Ben Blog | 10 September at 8.07 p.m.

From Tasmania, we headed right into the middle of Australia to see Uluru (it used to be called Ayers Rock). It's a massive block of **sandstone** and a **sacred** place for the Indigenous Australians. We arrived here at sunset when the rock was glowing red. What a sight!

BARKO'S BLOG-TASTIC AUSTRALIA FACTS
The Great Barrier Reef runs for more than 2,000 kilometres (1,243 miles) along the north-east coast and is the world's biggest **coral reef**. It's home to thousands of animals – more than 1,500 types of fish, for a start.

After we left Uluru, we thought we'd explore some more of the outback. It's covered in sandy and stony deserts and is one of the hottest, driest places on Earth. I'm here in the Simpson Desert looking for Big Red, a famous **sand dune**. It's thirsty work.

BARKO'S BLOG-TASTIC AUSTRALIA FACTS

This amazing animal is a duck-billed platypus. It lives in rivers and streams in eastern Australia. The duck-billed platypus uses its webbed feet for swimming. It scoops up worms and shellfish from the muddy riverbed with its leathery, duck-like bill.

City sights

Most Australians live in cities around the coast. Our next stop was Sydney, the biggest city in Australia. It's home to 4.5 million people and is a busy, lively place. Barko took this snap of me outside the Sydney Opera House, one of the most famous landmarks in the city.

12

BARKO'S BLOG-TASTIC AUSTRALIA FACTS

Canberra is the capital city of Australia. It was built from scratch in 1913. This is Parliament House where the Australian government meets. It was built in the shape of a **boomerang**.

G'day!

Many Australians have **ancestors** from Britain and Europe. Many other people have moved to Australia from New Zealand, China, India, Italy and Vietnam. The people in this photo are Indigenous Australians. They were the first people to live in Australia around 50,000 years ago.

BARKO'S BLOG-TASTIC AUSTRALIA FACTS
Most Australians speak English but with an Australian **accent** and their own words. I've been learning a few. "G'day" means "hello", "fair dinkum" means "that's true", and "ripper" means "great" or "fantastic".

In Australia, the school day usually lasts from 9 a.m. until 3.30 p.m. Most children wear uniforms, and need sunhats and suncream all summer. Some children who live deep in the Australian outback cannot get to school. They have to have their lessons by radio or online instead.

BARKO'S BLOG-TASTIC AUSTRALIA FACTS

People in the Australian outback often live a long way from hospital, so they call a flying doctor instead. The Royal Flying Doctor Service has around 60 planes and flies tens of thousands of kilometres every day.

AMBULANCE 6

AMBUL

BROOME
SUB CENTRE

Royal Flying Doctor Service

VH-KFN

We're in the city of Melbourne for Australia Day. It's when Australians remember the arrival of the first ships from England. People are cheering and waving Australian flags, as they wait for the parade to pass. Later, there's going to be a spectacular firework display in Docklands.

BARKO'S BLOG-TASTIC AUSTRALIA FACTS

The Indigenous Australians believe in a time called the Dreaming when their **ancestors** made the world. They remember this time with dance and music. This man is playing a traditional Indigenous Australian instrument called the **didgeridoo**.

19

Time for a barbie

Posted by: Ben Blog | 26 January at 6.14 p.m.

It had been a long day and we were hungry, so we headed down to the beach for a barbie (barbeque). Barko couldn't wait to sink his teeth into some juicy snags (sausages). I stuck to prawns and a burger, with **pavlova** for dessert.

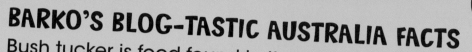

BARKO'S BLOG-TASTIC AUSTRALIA FACTS

Bush tucker is food found in the wild. The Indigenous Australians in the outback lived off it for thousands of years. Fancy tucking into goanna (lizard), honey ants or witchetty grubs? They're all on the bush tucker menu.

Mad about sport

Posted by: Ben Blog | 15 March at 2.30 p.m.

Staying in Melbourne, we've come to the Melbourne Cricket Ground to watch a game of Australian (Aussie) rules football. Players can kick, punch or pick up the ball, but throwing is not allowed. We're cheering for Hawthorn – one of Melbourne's top teams.

BARKO'S BLOG-TASTIC AUSTRALIA FACTS
Many Australians live near the sea, so swimming and surfing are very popular. There are brilliant surfing beaches around the country, like this one at Bells Beach. Surf's up, so I'm heading in.

From cattle stations to opal mines

Posted by: Ben Blog | 19 March at 7.53 a.m.

From Melbourne, we made our way west to the state of South Australia. We're spending a few days at Anna Creek cattle station, training to be jackaroos (cowboys). They've got around 17,000 cattle here. We'll be using trail bikes to round them up. Yikes!

BARKO'S BLOG-TASTIC AUSTRALIA FACTS

Shimmering gemstones called opals are one of Australia's most precious **natural resources**. They're mined here in Coober Pedy, a town in the Australian outback. It gets so hot in Coober Pedy that many people have also dug themselves homes underground.

And finally ...

The last stop on our tour was beautiful Rottnest Island off the coast of Western Australia. I wanted to see some quokkas. They are small, furry animals, about the size of cats. Quokkas are **marsupials**, like kangaroos and wallabies, and they're very rare. Here's a snap I took.

I am here!

BARKO'S BLOG-TASTIC AUSTRALIA FACTS
This is Sydney Harbour Bridge. It's nicknamed "the coathanger" because of its arch shape. You can climb to the top for a breathtaking view of the city, but you'll need a good head for heights.

Australia fact file

Area: 7,692,024 square kilometres
(2,969,907 square miles)

Population: 23,371,900 (2014)

Capital city: Canberra

Other main cities: Sydney, Melbourne, Brisbane

Language: English

Main religion: Christianity

Highest mountain: Mount Kosciuszko
(2,228 metres/7,310 feet)

Longest river: Murray River
(2,508 kilometres/1,558 miles)

Currency: Australian dollar

Australia quiz

Find out how much you know about Australia with our quick quiz.

1. What is Uluru made from?
a) opals
b) limestone
c) **sandstone**

2. What does "ripper" mean?
a) fantastic
b) rubbish
c) sunny

3. What is a **didgeridoo**?
a) an Australian drink
b) an Australian animal
c) an Australian musical instrument

4. What sport do Hawthorn play?
a) cricket
b) Aussie rules football
c) rugby

5. What is this?

Answers
1. c
2. a
3. c
4. b
5. Sydney Harbour Bridge

Glossary

accent way of speaking and pronouncing words

ancestor relative from the past

boomerang wooden, V-shaped object that was thrown for hunting

continent one of seven huge areas of land on Earth

coral reef long structure made from coral that grows along the coast

didgeridoo long, pipe-like musical instrument

inquisitive interested in learning about the world

Marco Polo explorer who lived from about 1254 to 1324. He travelled from Italy to China.

marsupial mammal with a pouch in which its babies grow

natural resource natural material that we use, such as coal, oil or wood

pavlova dessert made from meringue, topped with fruit and cream

sacred another word for holy, or special, to a person's religion or beliefs

sand dune giant heap of sand found in deserts and on beaches, piled up by the wind

sandstone soft rock that can be red, brown or grey

starvation death caused by lack of food

Find out more

Books

Australia (Countries Around the World), Mary Colson (Raintree, 2012)

Australia (Discover Countries), Chris Ward (Wayland, 2013)

Australia: Everything you ever wanted to know (Not For Parents) (Lonely Planet, 2013)

Websites

kids.nationalgeographic.co.uk/kids/places/find
National Geographic's website has lots of information, photos and maps of countries around the world.

www.kids-world-travel-guide.com/australia-facts.html
This website contains interesting Australia facts that have been chosen and researched by children especially for other children.

www.worldatlas.com
Packed with information about different countries, this website has flags, time zones, facts and figures, maps and timelines.

Index